EUTHANASIA

AND
ASSISTED SUICIDE

by
Philip H. Robinson

*All booklets are published thanks to the
generous support of the members of the
Catholic Truth Society*

CATHOLIC TRUTH SOCIETY
PUBLISHERS TO THE HOLY SEE

2

Contents

Acknowledgement

I wish to acknowledge the generous assistance of Professor Luke
Gormally with the writing of this booklet.

THE LINACRE CENTRE

The Linacre Centre is the only Catholic institution of its kind specialising in the field of healthcare ethics in Great Britain and Ireland. As such it provides a unique service to the Catholic community in these islands and more particularly to Catholics working in the field of healthcare. The Centre also exists to assist the teaching authorities within the Church in addressing bioethical issues, and to communicate and defend the Church's moral teaching in debates over public policy and legislation in the United Kingdom.

The Centre has built up a large bioethics library at the Hospital of St John and St Elizabeth in London. It has three fulltime research fellows who are able to give time and thought to new and difficult issues in bioethics and it is also able to call upon the help of a range of experts in medicine, law, philosophy, theology and history. The Centre is affiliated to the Ave Maria School of Law, Ann Arbor, Michigan. It publishes reports, organises conferences and lectures, and does consultancy work for individuals and for other organisations. The co-operation of the Linacre Centre in publishing the *CTS Explanations* series of booklets is intended to advance this work of providing clear Catholic teaching on bioethical issues.

INTRODUCTION

The purpose of this booklet is to explain the Church's teaching on euthanasia. In the past a booklet such as this would probably have been superfluous, since the attitude of Catholics to this issue would have been unequivocal and universal: unquestioned opposition. Today, however, some Catholics are finding it difficult to know what the Church teaches on this matter and how they, personally, should respond to difficult situations in their own lives. Medical advances and ambiguities in the law make it even more difficult for Catholics to understand how the straightforward teaching of the Church is to be applied in different situations. This is especially true when the supporters of euthanasia make appeals to what sound like Christian virtues, such as mercy, compassion and love.

This booklet will attempt not only to state with clarity the Church's teaching on euthanasia, but also, in a society that seeks to undermine this teaching both consciously and unconsciously, to defend it. It is the belief of this author, and of the Church, that the traditional teaching on euthanasia is the only one that is in accordance with a proper understanding of the human person. It is the only one that insists upon the value and inviolability of every human life, no matter how impaired that life may be. Because of this, it is the only one that is able to defend our society against the harmful and malicious intentions of the powers that would seek to destroy the weakest members in the name of progress or efficiency.

This is a bold assertion and one that seems insensitive to those who support euthanasia on compassionate grounds. Nevertheless, it is important that especially those people who view euthanasia as a natural consequence of their Christian convictions should realise that the arguments they use are corrosive of the values that preserve the rights of every member of society. By this is meant the rights not only of the healthy and productive but also the rights of the unborn, those with disabilities, the old and the sick. Only such a philosophy can be in accordance with the care that Our Lord Jesus Christ insists is due to "the least of these my brethren." (*Mt* 25:40, 45)

It is also the conviction of this author that the Church's teaching on euthanasia is essentially straightforward, although the application of this teaching in particular situations may be complex. To ensure that the teaching is as clear as possible it is important to begin with some definitions of the terms that will be used. It will also be helpful to try and understand the sorts of argument that are presented by those who are in favour of euthanasia. Most of these arguments are proffered in terms of a genuine concern to do what is right, which is why it is so important to understand clearly what those arguments are before we can understand why the Church wholly opposes them.

DEFINITION OF KEY TERMS

Suicide

In recent years advocates of euthanasia have increasingly taken to calling it 'assisted suicide'. They have tactical reasons for doing so (see p. 6) but the terminological move they make serves to obscure important differences between the issues raised by suicide and those raised by euthanasia, and in particular by proposals to legalise euthanasia. So a clear definition of suicide is needed. A standard dictionary[1] defines suicide as "the act or an instance of killing oneself intentionally." To do something 'intentionally' is to do it with a specific purpose. The dictionary definition does not make it wholly clear that one may accomplish the purpose of ending one's own life either by an act (e.g. taking poison) or by deliberately omitting to do what is required to preserve one's life (e.g. by starving oneself). It is important to the whole debate about suicide and euthanasia to be aware that some cases of omission resulting in death are morally equivalent to acts aimed at causing death. Some failures to do what one should do are also aimed at causing death. So what matters is the purpose or intention one has in mind in acting or failing to act.

Assisted suicide

Properly speaking one assists suicide if one assists a person to kill himself. What directly brings about the death is the deliberately adopted course of conduct of the person who is killed. The person who assists is answerable for 'assisting' and not for the actual killing. If one carries out the actual killing it ceases to be a case of 'assisting suicide'.

One may assist in suicide in a number of ways: by encouraging a person to kill himself, by advising him how to do it, by providing him with the means of doing it.

Euthanasia

The meaning of this key term has changed over time. The roots of the word are Greek in origin and it literally means 'good death' or a death that is free from suffering.

As currently understood, however, the term is typically defined in the following way:

> The act of killing someone painlessly, especially to relieve suffering from an incurable illness.[2]

In the Church's teaching it is defined as follows:

> Euthanasia in the strict sense is understood to be an action or omission which of itself and by intention causes death, with the purpose of eliminating all suffering.[3]

It is clear from both of these definitions that the key idea is that of a death that is caused intentionally, with the purpose of bringing an end to suffering.

In an important Working Party Report we find the following definition of euthanasia:

> ...there is euthanasia when the death of a human being is brought about on purpose as part of the medical care being given him.[4]

In this definition such killing is identified from the perspective of those who would like to see it as an integral part of ordinary health care. The Working Party amplified their brief definition as follows:

> ...in euthanasia a person's death is brought about on the ground that, because of his present or likely future mental condition and quality of life...it would be better for him...if that person were dead.[5]

This definition brings out a quite central point about euthanasia: euthanasia is typified by a decision to end a person's life based upon a judgement that the person's life is not worth living. The person killed is believed to be better off dead precisely because of the judgement that his suffering (or some other aspect of his condition) is so serious as to make his life no longer worthwhile. This is a key element in the thinking of people for whom euthanasia appears justified. And it is just this feature of their thinking to which the Church is emphatically opposed. So a central theme for our reflection will be whether there is such a thing as a life not worth living.

To summarise: euthanasia is the deliberate killing, by act or omission, of a person when death is deemed to be a medical benefit because it is judged that the person's life, because of his condition, is no longer worth living. Such reasons for deliberate killing will be referred to in what follows as 'euthanasiast reasons'.

Voluntary euthanasia

This is the intentional killing of a person for euthanasiast reasons carried out at the request of the person killed. Advocates of euthanasia would insist that the request should be free and informed. Underlying any such request, whether it is prompted by physical or psychological or spiritual suffering, is the sense that continued existence is no longer worthwhile.

Non-voluntary euthanasia

This is intentional killing for euthanasiast reasons carried out on those unable to request it because they lack the mental ability to do so; in legal terms, such patients are described as 'incompetent'. Non-voluntary euthanasia is carried out on a number of categories of incompetent patients: newborn babies who are seriously disabled; adults with mental disabilities; elderly people with dementia; and those in a permanent state of unconsciousness due to accident or illness.

Those who carry out non-voluntary euthanasia do so because they believe that the patients they kill would be better off dead. In so thinking they clearly take the view that the lives of these patients are no longer worthwhile.

Involuntary euthanasia

This is intentional killing for euthanasiast reasons carried out on people who are capable of asking for it but whose consent has either not been sought or has been refused.

Most advocacy of euthanasia does not include advocacy of killing which is either indifferent to or contrary to the wishes of competent patients. Nonetheless, such killing occurs in the belief that, whatever the person to be killed thinks, his or her life is in fact no longer worthwhile. If it is possible to make that kind of judgment then we should perhaps not be surprised that there are those who rely on it to 'justify' killing competent persons who do not wish to be killed.

A centrally important question to be addressed in this booklet is whether killing people can be justified on the basis of a judgment that their lives are not worthwhile.

We now turn to defining two terms around which a good deal of confusion gathers in debates about euthanasia. The two terms apply to euthanasia, whether it is voluntary, non-voluntary or involuntary.

Active euthanasia

This is the intentional bringing about of death for euthanasiast reasons by a positive act; for example, by injection with a lethal dose of poison.

Passive euthanasia

This is the intentional bringing about of death for euthanasiast reasons by omitting or failing to do something that should have been done; for example, by not feeding a patient in order that he will starve to death.

The term 'passive euthanasia' is used in this booklet to refer to neglect decided upon precisely in order to bring about a patient's death. It is important to realise that in much writing about our subject the term is used in a broader and rather confusing way to refer to any deliberate omission of treatment or care which has the effect of hastening death whether or not the hastening of death was intended. As we shall see, there can be perfectly good reasons for withholding or withdrawing treatments even when to do so has the effect of hastening death. It is confusing when the term 'passive euthanasia' is used to refer to both morally unacceptable and morally acceptable choices. It is important always to ask oneself what a person's immediate purpose is - what his *intention* is - in the choices he makes.

One effect of not recognising the key importance of intention has been the creation of a climate of opinion in which *any* hastening of death which results from the omission of treatment or care is regarded as acceptable, whether or not the purpose of the omission was to hasten death. This climate of opinion has now found expression in case law in England and Wales in which only active euthanasia is treated as unlawful.[6]

The Church recognises no morally significant distinction between actions and omissions which are alike in being chosen precisely to bring about death.

Advance directives and living wills

It is relevant to define these terms here for two reasons. First, because 'living wills' were pioneered in the USA by advocates of euthanasia as a way of advancing their cause. Secondly, because, unsurprisingly, they are legal instruments which may be used for euthanasiast purposes.

An advance directive is an instruction by a person as to what should happen if he or she becomes incompetent. Broadly speaking this instruction may take two forms.

One may confer on someone a continuing power of attorney, appointing another person to make decisions on one's behalf if one becomes incompetent. And clearly one can advise this person about one's preferences. At present powers of attorney in English (as opposed to Scottish) law do not extend to the area of healthcare, but the Government envisages legislation to enable them to do so.

Alternatively, one may make a 'living will', which is a written instruction as to what should, or should not, happen to one in the event of one's becoming incompetent. The most significant type of living will in connection with euthanasia is an advance refusal of treatment. This aims to make clear the kinds of treatment, or even care, that one would find unacceptable in certain circumstances. If an advance refusal of treatment is motivated by the belief that in certain circumstances (say of extreme dependency and weakness) life would be no longer worth living and one would be better off dead, then the refusal is suicidal: it is *aimed at* hastening one's death.

Footnotes

1. Collins Dictionary.

2. *Ibid.*

3. *Evangelium Vitae* 3, 65.

4. Luke Gormally (ed.) *Euthanasia, Clinical Practice and the Law*, London: The Linacre Centre 1994, p. 11.

5. *Ibid.*

6. The case which created this situation is the *Bland* case [1993]. For a discussion of this case, see Luke Gormally (ed.) *Euthanasia, Clinical Practice and the Law*. London: The Linacre Centre 1994, pp. 155-157.

ARGUMENTS PRESENTED IN
FAVOUR OF EUTHANASIA

The appeal to mercy

When we hear stories of terrible human suffering we feel
compassion both for those who suffer and for those who
have to witness the suffering of those whom they love.
Our minds, finding such suffering difficult to tolerate,
then seek ways to end this suffering. It is at this point that
euthanasia is usually suggested as a solution. Most people
would defend the practice of euthanasia by appealing to
our sense of mercy. We put animals out of their misery
when they suffer, why can we not do the same for
people? Why can we not extend this kindness to those we
love more than we could ever love a dog or a horse?

Before the Church's teaching on euthanasia is
presented it should be acknowledged that, while there are
often more insidious forces at work politically or socially,
many appeals for euthanasia, on the personal level, are
based upon a desire to do what is right and loving. The
most common argument advanced in favour of
euthanasia, both voluntary and non-voluntary, is the one
that says it is more merciful to kill people than to allow
them to go on suffering without release. While many who
say this are wholly concerned with the suffering of the

dying patient, pleas for mercy are sometimes prompted by the inability of relatives and others to accompany the dying person in his or her suffering; they are the expressions of a failure of compassion (which literally means 'suffering with') and courage.

The Church opposes the argument from 'mercy', not because it wishes to condemn people to a life of suffering, but rather because it recognises the danger of not drawing a distinction between human and animal life and because it recognises the damage that would be done to our view of human beings if it were ever held to be the case that a human life could become worthless.

The argument from self-determination

The second kind of argument that is usually presented in favour of voluntary euthanasia is one that bases itself on a certain idea of human rights. It is claimed that all human beings have a right to self-determination. By this is meant that all human beings have the right to decide what they do with their own lives. It is clear that some such right exists. But how far does the right extend? Advocates of euthanasia would take it to extend to the right of a person to choose when he or she dies. Sometimes this is spoken of as the 'right to die'. This term can be confusing. If all one means by the 'right to die' is the right to be allowed to die unburdened by futile and stressful treatments then there can be no objection to such a right. But advocates of euthanasia have more in mind than that. They think of the 'right to die' as a right to end one's own life at the time of one's choosing and the right to have others end one's life; in other words, by 'right to die' they mean 'right to be killed, by act or omission, at one's discretion'.

The claim that a right to self-determination extends to a right to be killed at one's discretion has a considerable appeal to many people today. In part this is because of a loss of belief in objective moral truths which have claims upon us; this belief has been replaced by the belief that everyone has to decide for himself what is to count as good and right. If this belief were true then it would indeed be down to each person to decide when his or her life ceased to be worthwhile, and when therefore he or she would be 'better off dead'. But as we shall see below there are sound reasons for recognising objective moral truths and for rejecting the idea that human lives may be judged to be not worthwhile.

The argument from quality of life

The third kind of argument that is often presented is one that has two distinct forms. In one of its forms it claims that at some points human life is so beset with suffering, indignity or hardship that it ceases to be worth living. People speak of a person's 'quality of life' and conclude that unless that life is of sufficient quality (something to be determined by a subjective decision) then it is not worth preserving or protecting.

The other form of this argument draws a distinction between 'human beings' and 'human persons'. In their common usage these terms are either thought of as having the same meaning, or at least a meaning which in its ordinary use refers to the same set of beings (namely, human beings), so that anyone who is a human being is also recognised as a person. However, some thinkers define 'person' in such a way that not every human being is a person. To be a 'person', it is said, one must possess certain developed psychological abilities. If a human being is alive but does not possess these abilities (eg. self-consciousness, the ability to reason clearly, the ability to form relationships) then that human being is not to be counted as a person. Personhood becomes something that you acquire and may lose rather than something that every living human being possesses. Only 'persons' in this sense, it is claimed, possess the rights that are listed in the Universal Declaration of Human Rights. Non-voluntary euthanasia may be advocated on the grounds that incompetent human beings, due to the impoverished state of their existence, have no right to life, since they have either not yet become 'persons' (being unborn, or babies, or mentally disabled) or have ceased to be 'persons' (being senile or permanently unconscious).

BELIEFS THAT UNDERPIN THE CHURCH'S TEACHING ON SUICIDE AND EUTHANASIA

The objective moral law

Among the many conflicts about the nature of morality, one is of particular importance in our day. The two sides of this conflict characterise almost all moral debate in the contemporary world. One of these views claims that there is no such thing as objective moral law. The 'rightness' and 'wrongness' of actions is different for different individuals, cultures and eras. This same view proclaims as its chief virtue tolerance of moral differences between people. It does not believe that a person can hold a wrong moral opinion, a view epitomised in the claim that "Everyone is entitled to their own opinion." Such a view is known as relativism. It is called relativism because its chief doctrine is that all morality is relative: there are no absolute laws that apply to every age and in all places - each age, each place invents its own. An appeal is made here to the laws and rules that have varied from culture to culture and from age to age. It is assumed that such changes demonstrate that the moral law cannot be something objective and universal. In this context, it is proposed to accept and legalise a practice such as euthanasia, that has been strongly disapproved of for most of the past 2000 years.

The Church wholly rejects such a moral stance and, amidst today's hostile moral climate, proclaims a truth concerning morality that is unpopular but essential to human well being. The truth the Church proclaims is that morality is not a human invention, nor a social convention but an unchanging and binding law. It teaches that the difference between right and wrong is something that is given; it is not something that is invented but something that is discovered. The moral law is part of the very nature of what makes people human. As St Paul states: "what the law requires is written on their hearts" (*Rom* 2:15).

This moral law, then, is something carved into the very heart of every human being, in the sense that we have a natural ability to recognise it. These laws are evident to the undistorted exercise of reason, as is their binding force. They are not arbitrary but are essential to the attainment of the happiness and fulfilment for which we were made. The danger of not following them is not so much the risk of damnation (though that is certainly a possibility) but rather the risk of damaging others and ourselves, by undermining the possibility of happiness in our lives. The keeping of the law is what brings total fulfilment and peace. When Our Lord is asked what must be done to inherit eternal life, he replies: "If you would enter life, keep the commandments" (*Mt* 19:17). Here the reference to eternal life is not only about heaven but also about the life of the soul, the true and deep happiness that can begin to be experienced even in this life.

We see echoed in the words of recent Conciliar and Papal documents the same insistence on the reality of such an objective and binding moral law:

> ...the supreme rule of life is the divine law itself, the eternal, objective and universal law by which God out of his wisdom and love arranges, directs and governs the whole world and the paths of the human community. God has enabled man to share in this divine law, and hence man is able under the gentle guidance of God's providence increasingly to recognize the unchanging truth.[7]

The Church, with St Paul, holds that every human being has an innate capacity to recognise this law, which in that sense is something to be found 'written' on his or her own heart. There is therefore something 'unnatural' about failure to recognise this law or denial of its existence.

This law is not designed for the thwarting of our freedom and desires, but is part of God's love for all people. The law is itself a gift:

> God's commandment is never detached from his love: it is always a gift meant for man's growth and joy. As such, it represents an essential and indispensable aspect of the Gospel, actually becoming 'gospel' itself: joyful good news.[8]

This is because to disobey the law - at least wilfully - is to sin. Sin poisons those who commit it and causes pain to those who suffer it. Ultimately, rather than being an expression of freedom, it enslaves those who succumb to it. All people are called to obedience, for in that obedience is freedom, happiness and life. For the law corresponds to our nature. To ignore it is to ignore the purpose for which human beings were made.

In what is to come, it is taken for granted that in discussions of right and wrong, there is such a thing as an objective moral law. There are many arguments to demonstrate the truth of this claim that do not rely on the arguments of scripture nor do they presume any faith commitment.[9]

The Church's moral teaching proceeds on the understanding that there is an objective moral law. For the believer this is recognised as the law of God, since it exists in virtue of God's intentions in creating us as the kind of creature we are. Since we have a natural capacity to recognise this law - namely our reason - the rationally discoverable content of God's law is referred to as the Natural Law. The Church holds that even those who do not believe in God are capable of recognising the objective and binding force of the moral law. Neither the believer, nor the unbeliever can escape its demands.

The value and inviolability of every human life

The Church affirms the existence of universal and absolute moral laws. One of these laws is the prohibition against killing innocent human beings. This law has a positive correlative. The law prohibiting the killing of the innocent exists because every human life is valuable. It does not matter how impaired this life may be; whether it is beset with suffering, disability, ignorance or even sin, it remains, in its own self, something of great value. Therefore, it demands protection and it needs to be defended against malicious attack. The dignity of every human being is therefore unconditional. It cannot be revoked or transgressed. That is what is meant by the inviolability of human life. When the Church speaks of this preciousness and inviolability of human life, it uses the word sacred. Human life is valuable because it is ascribed a unique and irrevocable dignity by its Creator. As Pope John Paul II says:

> "Life is always a good. This is an instinctive perception and a fact of experience, and man is called to grasp the profound reason why this is so...This question is found everywhere in the Bible, and from the very first pages it receives a powerful and amazing answer. The life which God gives man is quite different from the life of all other living creatures, inasmuch as man, although formed from the dust of the earth (cf. *Gen* 2:7, 3:19; *Job* 34:15; *Ps* 103:14; 104:29), is a manifestation of God in the world, a sign of his presence, a trace of his glory (cf. *Gen* 1:26-27; *Ps* 8:6)... Man has been given a sublime dignity, based on the intimate bond which unites him to his Creator: in man there shines forth a reflection of God himself."[10]

It is the fact that human life is made in God's image that gives it its unique worth. That is why the killing of an innocent human being is murder and the killing of other animals, although in certain circumstances morally questionable, never carries the same moral gravity as murder.

The Church teaches that the inviolability of human life is a truth of the natural law; so it ought to be possible to commend it on the basis of reasons which even a non-believer could accept. The truth that the Church expresses when it says that man is made in the image of God is recognised by all people. It is the truth that the difference between humans and even the highest animals is not a mere difference in degree but a difference in kind. This truth has been partially obscured by thinking of humans as the end point of an evolutionary development, as a particularly advanced sort of animal. The fact that human beings are a kind of animal life is not a startling revelation. What is startling, given that we share many traits with the animals, are the ways in which we differ from them. There are no animals that produce art or literature; there are no animals that communicate through abstract forms of language; there are no animals that adorn themselves with clothes or prepare their food; there are no animals that indulge in architecture, drama, debate, politics, philosophy or law; there are no animals who can feel guilt and express moral outrage. Similarly there are no animals that wage war on other animals, or perform wilful acts of cruelty and torture, or delight in exploiting others for their own pleasure. As G.K. Chesterton said, human beings exceed the animals by the measure of heaven and hell. What these phenomena point to are the natural capacities which explain them and which make for the distinctiveness of human beings: rationality and the freedom of the will.

Thus human beings are unlike all other living creatures. They have a unique dignity due to the potentiality that belongs to them as proper to their nature. It is for this reason that the taking of a human life is considered so grievous:

> The sacredness of life gives rise to its inviolability, written from the beginning in man's heart, in his conscience... in the depths of his conscience, man is always reminded of the inviolability of life - his own life and that of others - as something which does not belong to him, because it is the property and gift of God the Creator and Father.[11]

And even if the non-believer does not recognise the ownership of God he must at least recognise that human beings cannot arbitrarily deprive each other of life since they must recognise the distinctive value, and therefore dignity, of each human being, which he or she possesses because of his or her human nature.

Every human being is a person

Some contemporary philosophers deny that human dignity belongs to all human beings, distinguishing (as we have already seen) between lives that are merely human and those which are distinctively 'personal'. A human life becomes and remains 'personal', according to these philosophers, only when it acquires and retains abilities for understanding and choice and for self-consciously entering into personal relationships. Only human beings with such acquired abilities are to be counted as 'persons', and only 'persons' (so defined) should be thought of as possessing human rights. This means that, for those who hold this position, unborn babies, infants and very young children, people with severe mental disabilities, and those with senile dementia, do not possess basic human rights, such as the right not to be unjustly killed. They are simply not entitled to justice.

The Church rejects this false dichotomy between the human being and the human person. The Church professes that all human beings are persons who share the same rights and the same dignity as individual members of the human race:

> "...how could a human individual not be a human person?"[12]

Two considerations should persuade us that the basis of human dignity is our nature rather than acquired abilities. The first consideration is that we are able to acquire abilities for understanding and choice and the like only because of a fundamental capacity inherent in the nature we have as humans. If we acknowledge that a special worth and dignity attaches to certain developed abilities then an even more fundamental dignity attaches to the nature in virtue of which we possess them.

The second consideration concerns the link between dignity, rights and entitlement to just treatment. The entitlement of human beings to just treatment cannot be something which is determined on an arbitrary basis, for arbitrariness is incompatible with justice. But it *will be* determined arbitrarily if it is made to depend on the dignity which attaches to acquired abilities. Even if there is agreement on which are the relevant acquired abilities, what level of developed ability must somebody acquire before being entitled to just treatment? If it is said, as some do say, that human beings must be able to think of themselves as 'selves' with a future in order to be counted as persons, the requirement seems arbitrary on two counts. First, why that requirement rather than others? Second, given that most young human beings who have not yet acquired that way of thinking are capable of doing so, it seems quite arbitrary to treat them as non-persons. The only way of being non-arbitrary about who are entitled to be treated justly is to recognise the equality in basic dignity which belongs to us simply in virtue of the fact that we are human.

The Church does not recognise any defence of euthanasia that rests upon the assessment of a particular individual's life as worthless. There is no illness, pain or loss of capacity that can render a person's life not worthwhile and therefore disposable. Such a judgement on a person's life is incompatible with recognition of the dignity that every human being possesses.[13]

We are stewards and not owners

A further consideration advanced in defence of euthanasia is the idea that the right to self-determination is one that must include the right to end one's own life. The claim is that since this is my life then I can do with it what I please and even bring it to a premature end.

The Church rejects such an argument primarily because it does not believe that man's power over his own life is a power due to ownership but rather a power attached to stewardship. As John Paul II says:

Man's lordship however is not absolute, but ministerial: it is a real reflection of the unique and infinite lordship of God.[14]

That is to say, life belongs to man rather in the way that a child belongs to his parents. The child is not their property but their special charge. They have responsibility for the child but no rights in relation to the child contrary to the life and well-being of the child. The faulty inference in the claim that "It is my life! So I can do what I like with it" perhaps arises from confusion over the meaning of the word 'my'. The word 'my' sometimes implies ownership, as in 'my shoes' (where ownership means they are at my disposal); sometimes it implies a distinctive relationship, such as that between husband and wife ('my husband', 'my wife'), in which, though people have particular claims on each other, they are not each other's property; and sometimes it expresses the idea of belonging to something else (as in 'my team, my school, my country' or even, 'my God') in which the something or somebody else controls the terms on which I belong. The use of the word 'my' does not on its own entail that one has rights over the thing claimed as one's own. My relationship to 'my life' has to be understood in the light of the fact that each of us belongs in a fundamental way to God. None of us has the right to end his or her own life, because God controls the terms on which we have life.

Human life is sacred because from its beginning it involves the creative action of God, and it remains forever in a special relationship with the Creator, who is its sole end. God alone is the Lord of life from its beginning until its end: no one can, in any circumstance, claim for himself the right to destroy directly an innocent human being.[15]

This is, of course, a religious argument. But even someone who does not believe in God can recognise that it trivialises human life to regard and treat it as disposable property.

The meaning of suffering

There is one other assumption that many of the arguments in favour of euthanasia make: that suffering is always an evil and something that human beings must avoid at all costs. This too is rejected by the Church. While it is true that suffering is an evil, which we often have a duty to combat, it can become a means of sanctification and a source of solidarity with others:

> Living to the Lord...means recognising that suffering, while still an evil and a trial in itself, can always become a source of good. It becomes such if it is experienced for love and with love through sharing, by God's gracious gift and one's own personal and free choice, in the suffering of Christ Crucified. In this way, the person who lives his suffering in the Lord grows more fully conformed to him (cf. *Phil* 3:10; *1 Pet* 2:21) and more closely associated with his redemptive work on behalf of the Church and humanity.[16]

There is a deep mystery here that the world increasingly fails to recognise. True love is most forcibly expressed through sacrifice - this is often not the sacrifice that gives up life but the sacrifice that is willing to suffer for the sake of others or for the sake of testimony to a higher truth. Of course, such suffering cannot be imposed, but those who suffer can willingly offer their suffering and therefore bear witness to their complete acceptance of the inviolable dignity of human life.

The argument that presents euthanasia as a form of mercy misunderstands not only the place of suffering in human life but also the role of those who care for the one who suffers. It is certainly a very peculiar use of the word 'mercy' that considers it appropriate in the name of eliminating suffering to eliminate the one who suffers:

> ...euthanasia must be called a *false mercy*, and indeed a disturbing 'perversion' of mercy. True 'compassion' leads to sharing another's pain; it does not kill the person whose suffering we cannot bear.[17]

The Church presumes there is something worse than suffering; that is, the denial of the dignity a person has as a human being by intentionally destroying that person's life on the grounds that it is no longer worthwhile. Proper love for another person ought to lead us to a patient and willing 'suffering-with' that person. When pain cannot be removed it must be borne and it is precisely then that those who love the person most can demonstrate their presence to them in their most needy hour. This 'suffering-with' is the true and literal meaning of the word compassion.

Footnotes

7. Vatican Council II, Declaration on Religious Freedom *Dignitatis Humanae*, 3.

8. *Evangelium Vitae*, 52.

9. For an accessible exposition of some arguments against relativism see C.S. Lewis, *The Abolition of Man*.

10. *Evangelium Vitae*, 34.

11. *Ibid.* 40.

12. Congregation for the Doctrine of the Faith, Instruction on Respect for Human Life in its Origin and on the Dignity of Procreation *Donum Vitae* (22 February 1987), I, No. 1: *AAS* 80 (1988), 78-79.

13. See Luke Gormally (ed.), *Euthanasia, Clinical Practice and the Law*. London: The Linacre Centre 1994, especially pp. 119-126.

14. John Paul II *Evangelium Vitae* 3, 52.

15. Congregation for the Doctrine of the Faith, Instruction on Respect for Human Life in its Origin and on the Dignity of Procreation *Donum Vitae* (22 February 1987), I, No. 1: *AAS* 80 (1988), 76-77.

16. John Paul II, *Evangelium Vitae* 3, 67. When we come to discuss some of the ethical issues in relation to pain control (see pp. 49-56), we should remember that a patient may desire to forgo analgesia precisely to offer his or her sufferings in union with the sufferings of Christ. Such a choice obviously has to be the free choice of the patient concerned.

17. *Ibid.* 66.

THE CHURCH'S TEACHING ON SUICIDE AND EUTHANASIA AND ITS IMPLICATIONS

Suicide

The Church has always taught that suicide, understood as the ending of one's own life by a course of conduct chosen with that end in view, is seriously wrong. It is a contravention of the fifth commandment ("Thou shall not kill"; see *Ex* 20:13; *Deut* 5:17). It shows a lack of proper love for self, which is commanded implicitly in Our Lord's injunction to "love your neighbour as yourself" (*Mk* 12:31). It also shows a lack of consideration for the duties that are owed to others in the community, especially immediate family, and a lack of regard for the effect it will have upon them. Finally, "in its deepest reality ... [it] represents a rejection of God's absolute sovereignty over life and death".[18]

Having said that, the Church does not condemn individuals who commit suicide because it recognises that often there are social or psychological pressures that may well mean that the person is not fully responsible for his or her actions. Indeed, it is difficult to imagine anyone in a healthy frame of mind who would willingly take his or her own life. We find this summed up in the words of Pope John Paul II:

Suicide is always as morally objectionable as murder. The Church's tradition has always rejected it as a gravely evil choice. Even though a certain psychological, cultural and social conditioning may induce a person to carry out an action which so radically contradicts the innate inclination to life, thus lessening or removing subjective responsibility, suicide, when viewed objectively, is a gravely immoral act.[19]

Many (but not all) suicides bear a fundamental similarity to euthanasia, in that people who commit suicide frequently do so because of an explicit or implicit judgment that their lives are no longer worthwhile.

Assistance in suicide

Assistance in suicide exists when a person aids and abets another person to take his or her own life. Obviously, Jack can assist Jill to commit suicide only if Jill is intent on *killing herself*. It is not assistance in suicide if *Jack* kills Jill at Jill's request; that is voluntary euthanasia. One of the ways in which contemporary debate about voluntary euthanasia is being systematically confused is by calling voluntary euthanasia 'assisted suicide'. Proponents of the legalisation of voluntary euthanasia in the UK have adopted this piece of linguistic subterfuge partly because they like to argue along the following lines. (1) Since 1961 suicide has not been a criminal offence in England and Wales. Therefore (2) suicide is lawful. So (3) people have a right to commit suicide. Therefore (4), if, because of physical or other impediments, they cannot kill themselves, they should be entitled to have someone kill them. To provide such help would amount to assisting someone to bring about his own death; it would be 'assisted suicide'. In reality, of course, it would be euthanasia. (2), (3) and (4) are indefensible.

The fact that the Suicide Act of 1961 decriminalised suicide does not mean that suicide is lawful. All it means is that people who make failed suicide attempts will not be prosecuted. It was made clear by the Government of the time that it introduced a bill to decriminalise suicide because people who attempt suicide and fail need medical and psychiatric help rather than a prosecution, which is likely to intensify their suicidal feelings. But the Act makes it clear that suicide continues to be unlawful behaviour, by stipulating very heavy penalties (up to 14 years imprisonment) for assisting suicide. So it is a piece of groundless rhetoric to talk about a 'right to suicide' entailing a 'right to be assisted' to commit suicide.

The above is the legal situation, the truth about which is frequently ignored or suppressed by advocates of the legalisation of euthanasia. Whatever the legal situation is or may become, the moral truth about assisting in suicide is clear from the grave wrongness of suicide itself. One should never act in a way that aims to assist another in doing wrong. And if the wrongdoing one is assisting is grave then one's assistance is gravely wrong. "To concur with the intention of another person to commit suicide and to help in carrying it out through so-called 'assisted suicide' means to cooperate in, and at times to be the actual perpetrator of, an injustice which can never be excused, even if requested."[20]

Voluntary euthanasia

Pope John Paul II sees advocacy of euthanasia in contemporary society as rooted in two attitudes which are widespread in our age: the view that human lives can cease to be meaningful and worthwhile, and the view that human beings are completely free to dispose of their lives as they will: the view that we enjoy completely autonomous control over our lives. The first view, as we have seen, is incompatible with recognition of the dignity which belongs to every human being simply in virtue of the fact that he or she is a human being (see pp. 20-23 above). The second view is incompatible with recognition of the fact that our lives are gifts of God of which we are stewards, not owners (see pp. 26-27 above).

Even if a person rejects the idea that we enjoy only stewardship of our lives, a claim to complete autonomy will not suffice as a plausible justification even for *voluntary* euthanasia. Bear in mind that euthanasia, as distinct from suicide, involves someone other than the person who is to die carrying out the killing; in most schemes for legalising euthanasia it is proposed that doctors should perform it. That means that it is the doctor who is answerable for the death of the patient. A doctor cannot plausibly justify his killing of a patient by relying on the mere wish or demand of the patient to be killed. Something more needs to be said to make that wish or demand seem reasonable. And the 'something more' ("I'm suffering unbearable pain"; "I feel hopeless"; "I cannot bear the indignity of the dependency I now experience"; "I've nothing more to live for") really comes down to the patient's belief that his life is no longer worthwhile. Since, however, the doctor who is to do the killing is the person answerable for it, he must *share* the patient's view of his life as no longer worthwhile. If he disagrees with the patient's view of his life then he is without even the *appearance* of a justification for carrying out the killing. The belief or judgment that someone's life is no longer worthwhile carries the main burden of purporting to justify even voluntary euthanasia.

It is because the Church knows the truth about the dignity of *every* human being and therefore holds that no human life, however impaired, can be devoid of worth, that she teaches the wrongness of euthanasia. Pope John Paul II solemnly confirmed the binding and unchangeable character of this teaching when he declared:

...in harmony with the Magisterium of my Predecessors and in communion with the Bishops of the Catholic Church, *I confirm that euthanasia is a grave violation of the law of God*, since it is the deliberate and morally unacceptable killing of a human person. This doctrine is based upon the natural law and upon the written word of God, is transmitted by the Church's tradition and taught by the ordinary and universal Magisterium.[21]

Non-voluntary and involuntary euthanasia

Non-voluntary euthanasia is the killing of a patient who is incapable of asking to be killed (because too young or too mentally impaired). Involuntary euthanasia is the killing of a patient who is mentally competent and who has either shown no desire to be killed or who has made it clear that he does not wish to be killed. It may surprise readers that involuntary euthanasia occurs. But Government statistics from Holland, which have significantly understated the incidence of euthanasia[22], nonetheless make it clear that involuntary euthanasia has occurred there.

Of course, doctors who carry out non-voluntary and involuntary euthanasia believe they are benefiting those they kill by putting an end to lives that are no longer worth living. Once one believes that the lives of some human beings are not worthwhile - a belief basic to the 'justification' of voluntary euthanasia - and that these human beings would therefore be better off dead, it can hardly seem reasonable to withhold the 'benefit' of being killed from those incapable of requesting it (non-voluntary euthanasia). It may seem to require a particular arrogance, however, for doctors to decide that there are competent patients who fail to recognise that death is in their best interests and so fail to ask for what they need. Yet, if a doctor thinks that it is possible to judge that a human life is not worthwhile he presumably thinks there are 'objective criteria' for reaching that judgment, criteria of the kind he employs in the case of the incompetent. If one assumes the existence of such criteria, a doctor may judge that they are satisfied in the case of a competent patient who does not request euthanasia.

It will be obvious that the Church's teaching that euthanasia "is a grave violation of the law of God", which was quoted in the previous section, applies as much to non-voluntary and involuntary euthanasia as it does to voluntary euthanasia.

Footnotes

18. John Paul II, *Evangelium Vitae* 66.

19. *Ibid.*

20. *Ibid.*

21. *Evangelium Vitae* 65.

22. On under-reporting of euthanasia practice in Holland, see John Keown, *Euthanasia, Ethics and Public Policy*. Cambridge: Cambridge University Press 2002, pp. 81-149 *passim*. On involuntary euthanasia see p. 104.

NEGATIVE AND POSITIVE DUTIES

Negative and positive duties and the prolongation of life

The duty *not* to aim to cause the death of the innocent is absolute; that is, it does not admit of exceptions. It does not admit of exceptions because no exceptions one might make could be compatible with justice. People sometimes seek to explain the absolute character of this negative duty by saying that human life is an absolute value. Here the word 'absolute' is being used to suggest that human life is a supreme value, and that all choices should somehow be subordinate to our remaining alive. The claim is mistaken. Human life is indeed a 'basic value', meaning a value which is fundamental to human well-being, and which therefore underlies many of the choices we make in the conduct of our lives. If Jack says "I leapt that fence when I saw the bull charging across the field because I feared for my life", we don't find puzzling the thought that Jack wanted to preserve his life. There could hardly be a more obviously basic ingredient of human well-being than being alive along with being in fairly good condition. But human life is not the only basic good. Physicists spend a large part of their lives trying to discover the truth about the physical universe. Historians devote time to discovering the truth about past human societies. Theologians work to understand and relate to each other the truths given to us in revelation. And truth is not just a basic good in the lives of 'intellectuals': all of us need to know many truths, and to avoid being confused and muddled and misled by false beliefs, if we are to live well as human beings. Friendship - namely, the commitment of persons to treating the good of the other as their own good, and so seeking to achieve it - is also a basic good. A life without friendship is an impoverished life. Health is a basic good: the good which explains the choices we should make to take proper care of ourselves, as well as the good which explains the fundamental commitment of doctors and nurses and other health professionals.

The existence of a *plurality* of basic goods - the ones just mentioned and others - means that while there is a plurality of absolute *negative* duties (choices we should never make) designed to preserve respect for the values basic to our well-being and the well-being of others, there are no absolute *positive* duties: choices we should always make to promote a particular basic good or value. One reason for this is that the positive promotion of one basic good can involve breach of an absolute negative duty to respect another basic good. There are scientists who sometimes talk as if the advancement of scientific knowledge justified, for example, destructive experimentation on human embryos. But innocent human lives are never to be intentionally destroyed, however worthwhile the purpose one may have in mind in doing so. Another example of active promotion of a good being rendered morally impossible by an absolute negative duty comes from the lives of many martyrs. Recognition of the duty not to deny the truth meant that they could not adopt any and every means to prolong their lives.

There are other reasons why we may not be obliged to seek to prolong either our own life or the life of another.

One is that sooner or later all of us have to die. When the dying process is irreversible we should bear in mind that the person dying needs to die well. So he or she needs to be provided, if it can be managed, with a relatively undisturbed environment offering the possibility of recollection. Many dying persons may need to make their peace with God, with family, or with others from whom they have been estranged. In these circumstances, medical treatment aimed at prolonging life, which will often be intensive and highly intrusive if the patient is dying, will be contrary to the dying person's most important needs. Dying patients need to be allowed to die well.

A second reason for holding that there is no absolute obligation to seek to prolong life is that attempts to do so can impose excessive burdens. Treatment can be excessively painful, cause excessive psychological stress, or impose excessive social and economic burdens. In general, we are *required* to be heroic only in circumstances in which failure to do so would involve us in breach of an absolute negative duty. The general obligation to care for and preserve one's life is merely a positive duty, which does not apply in all cases.

Even if the burdens consequent on medical treatment are not absolutely unbearable, if the treatment promises little in the way of increased life-span then there is hardly any warrant for considering it a matter of obligation to bear those burdens.

A third reason why there may be no obligation to seek to prolong life when one is dying is that it can be wholly reasonable to prefer life without life-prolonging treatment to life with such treatment. Think, for example, of an elderly woman with terminal cancer. The doctors tell her that with chemotherapy she can probably live for a further eighteen months; without chemotherapy she is likely to die in about six months. Chemotherapy will involve her having to make frequent stays in hospital, and the side-effects of treatment are likely to be very unpleasant. If she declines chemotherapy she can spend the remaining months of her life cared for in the household of her daughter, son-in-law and their children. The old woman declines chemotherapy because she prefers to spend her final months undisturbed in the loving environment of her daughter's family rather than suffering the distressing physical consequences of the proposed treatment along with the psychological stress and social dislocation of regular hospitalisation. Note that the woman's choice is not dictated by a desire to shorten her life but by the realisation that one way of living out her remaining days is far more attractive than the alternative. Her choice is dictated by a *positive* preference for the constant company of her daughter, son-in-law and grandchildren.

What has been explained so far in this section provides the background to the Church's teaching, which distinguishes between euthanasia, on the one hand, and reasonably founded decisions not to prolong life. And so Pope John Paul teaches:

Euthanasia must be distinguished from the decision to forego so-called 'aggressive medical treatment', in other words, medical procedures which no longer correspond to the real situation of the patient, either because they are by now disproportionate to any expected results or because they impose an excessive burden on the patient and his family. In such situations, when death is clearly imminent and inevitable, one can in conscience 'refuse forms of treatment that would only secure a precarious and burdensome prolongation of life, so long as the normal care due to the sick person in similar cases is not interrupted.'[23] Certainly there is a moral obligation to care for oneself and to allow oneself to be cared for, but this duty must take account of concrete circumstances. It needs to be determined whether the means of treatment available are objectively proportionate to the prospects for improvement. To forego extraordinary or disproportionate means is not the equivalent of suicide or euthanasia; it rather expresses acceptance of the human condition in the face of death.[24]

It should be clear from this teaching that there is no truth in the common accusation that respect for the sanctity or inviolability of human life requires a relentless and cruel commitment to prolonging life whatever the circumstances.

Ordinary and extraordinary means of prolonging life

In the quotation from *Evangelium Vitae* Pope John Paul II refers to 'extraordinary means' of prolonging life, which are contrasted with 'ordinary means'. The terms 'ordinary' and 'extraordinary', in the context of the Church's moral teaching, have a distinctive meaning, corresponding to the distinction between what one has an obligation to accept as a patient and treatment one has no obligation to accept. Within 'ordinary means' there is an important distinction to be made between medical *treatment* and *basic care*.

Treatments are 'ordinary' (i.e. obligatory) means of prolonging life if they are likely to be successful, carry no great risks, do not impose excessive burdens on the patient, and can be given without preventing the patient from attending to some other over-riding duty.

Basic care - namely, the provision of food and fluids, shelter, warmth, and necessary hygiene measures - is nearly always 'ordinary means' of prolonging life, i.e. means which carers have an obligation to provide and patients an obligation to accept. Why? Because as far as carers are concerned, provision of care measures is a fundamental expression of respect for the life entrusted to one's care; and, as far as patients are concerned, acceptance of such care is a fundamental expression of respect for the gift of one's own life. Food and fluids, in particular, are not medical *treatments*, which one might stop because they are no longer serving their purpose of curing a disease or alleviating symptoms. Food and fluids are simply intended to sustain life. There may be circumstances in which the way one has to deliver food and fluids becomes intolerable to the patient. This may become evident, for example, from the fact that a patient keeps pulling out the naso-gastric tube which has been inserted to keep him nourished. But in most circumstances you would not withhold food and fluids, which you were in a position to provide, unless you had the euthanasiast intention of hastening the patient's death.

Treatments are 'extraordinary', (i.e. not obligatory), if they offer a poor likelihood of success, carry high risks of causing death or damage (sometimes the case with experimental therapies), impose excessive burdens on the patient, or cannot be given without preventing the patient from attending to some undeniably important and over-riding duty.

If the reader reflects on what has just been said about 'ordinary and extraordinary' treatments it will be clear that it cannot correspond to a straightforward distinction between medical *treatments*, holding good for everyone. The distinction is relative both to the condition of patients and to developments in medicine. It is relative to the condition of patients because what one person finds burdensome is not necessarily found burdensome by another. And it is relative to developments in medicine because procedures which may be extremely risky at one time or in one place are much safer and successful later or may already be much safer in another place because of the resources available there.

The above offers a brief statement on the positive duties, both of patients and of healthcare professionals, when they face choices about treatment and care when lives are at risk. A fuller explanation of those duties is offered in another booklet in this series.[25]

Since the topics of this booklet are euthanasia and assisted suicide, we need to discuss duties to patients (and the duties of patients when competent) in two kinds of situation in which euthanasia characteristically takes place: in the care of the disabled newborn, and in terminal care (i.e. the care of patients with conditions from which they are dying). The discussion will be directed to answering some of the questions about what is morally acceptable and what is unacceptable in the care of the disabled newborn and in terminal care.

Euthanasia and the disabled newborn

Babies can be born with lethal conditions which can be corrected using well-established, generally successful procedures. For example, babies may be born with an intestinal obstruction (duodenal atresia), which uncorrected will lead to the death of the baby and which pediatric surgeons would not hesitate to correct if the baby had no other medical condition. However, if the baby is also born with a permanent disability (for example, with Down's syndrome), along with the duodenal atresia, parents have refused consent for the surgery and surgeons have gone along with or even encouraged the refusal. When this kind of thing happens people are apt to talk about 'letting nature take its course'.

But why is consent to surgery refused? It is because the parents do not want a Down's syndrome baby. They would rather have the baby dead than bear the responsibilities of caring for him or her. The surgery itself would clearly be beneficial to the child and would not carry with it particularly burdensome consequences. So in circumstances in which such surgery is readily available it is owing to the child. The decision to withhold the surgery is a euthanasiast decision: it is intended to ensure the death of the child.

This example of a Down's syndrome baby born with duodenal atresia helps to illustrate the importance of the distinction between asking whether *treatment* is worthwhile and asking whether *the life of the patient* is worthwhile. If we have a true understanding of human dignity we will not even ask the latter question.

What has been said here is not meant to imply that efforts to correct lethal conditions should be made in the case of all children born with such conditions. Sometimes babies are born with multiple lethal conditions, at least one of which is not correctable and will lead to the death of the child in a short period of time. In such circumstances surgery to correct the correctable conditions would bring too little benefit to the child and would likely impose considerable burdens on a very fragile body. So surgery would not be worthwhile.

There has been plenty of evidence of the euthanasiast killing of babies born with non-lethal disabilities, particularly those associated with spina bifida.[26] Such babies have been heavily sedated so that they are rendered largely incapable of crying out for the food and fluids they need. In consequence they die of dehydration and starvation. It is linguistic mystification to call such a policy 'letting nature take its course'. The policy is euthanasiast: it is *intended* to bring about the death of the babies.

Terminal care

People commonly think of euthanasia as a solution to the problem of patients who are dying in pain. Over the past forty years there have been impressive developments in the terminal care of patients. Given the use of modern approaches to pain control the vast majority of patients can be relieved of pain while still remaining conscious.

Techniques of pain control have themselves given rise to ethical questions which need to be answered in a booklet devoted to the topic of euthanasia. One question concerns the possible hastening of death caused by giving opiates (morphine) to control pain. Another question concerns an approach to pain control called 'terminal sedation' which is being increasingly advocated today.

Drugs that may hasten death and the doctrine of double effect

An opiate drug such as morphine depresses the respiratory centre of the brain along with other parts of the central nervous system. Hence a very large dose of morphine given to a patient whose body has not progressively adapted to the drug through steadily increasing doses is apt to kill the patient. Ideally pain control should begin well before pain becomes intolerable so that the patient can gradually adapt to increasing doses of morphine if they are necessary. If adequate morphine is administered at appropriate intervals the pain will remain under control. When pain is well-controlled in this way a patient's life is more likely to be prolonged rather than shortened by the use of morphine.

Unfortunately, patients are not always provided with adequate pain control when they begin to need it. Pain is allowed to get seriously out of control. At that point modest doses of morphine may no longer be adequate. But large doses may hasten death. Would it be wrong to administer such a dose knowing that it is possible that in doing so one would be hastening the patient's death?

The short answer to this question is: No, provided that your aim or intention is to control the pain, and that it is no part of your intention to hasten death. In other words, if you employ the morphine for its pain relieving potential, and you are not aiming to end the pain by ending the patient's life, then giving the drug in the required dose is morally acceptable. Of course, you will also need to ensure that the benefits of giving the morphine are sufficient to justify the risk of hastening death as a side-effect of treating the pain.

This answer is a particular application of a more generally applicable moral teaching known as **the doctrine of double effect**. As a guide to decision-making, the doctrine of double effect states a way of distinguishing between morally permissible and morally impermissible courses of action that are foreseen to have two effects, one good, one bad. It requires that what one chooses to do (what one *intends*), in the first instance, should be a good or morally neutral kind of action, that the good effect sought should not be brought about precisely through the choice of the bad effect, that the bad effect should be an unintended side effect, and that the good one is aiming to achieve should be sufficient to justify doing what causes (or risks) the bad effect.

What underlies the doctrine of double effect?

First, and most obviously, the truth that there are moral absolutes, i.e. *types* of act we should never choose to do. A type of act is identified by the intention with which we act. So if my chosen means or end is the death of an innocent person what I am choosing to do is, morally speaking, an act of murder.

Secondly, in committing myself to carrying out a wrong kind of act, I do not merely wrong another person (if another person is affected by what I do), I also corrupt myself. How? By making myself more disposed to behave in that way. If I lie I am more disposed to being a liar; if I rob I am more disposed to being a robber; if I carry out an abortion I am more disposed to being an abortionist. Of course, if I repent of such acts my dispositions can change.

Thirdly, we cause, or run the risk of causing, much more than we aim to bring about. Sometimes the importance or necessity of what we aim to bring about provides a valid excuse for, say, risking or causing death. And so a surgeon may embark on high risk experimental surgery in order to save a patient's life. In the event, the surgery has the not unexpected outcome of killing the patient. It was nonetheless justified because it offered the only chance - however slim - of saving the patient's life. Another example: mines rescue workers faced with the necessity of halting the spread of fire in one underground tunnel leading to others may have to block it off, thereby preventing any possibility of escape for miners caught behind the fire.

Fourthly (and paralleling the second point) what we cause but do not aim to bring about we are not *committed* to achieving. And the absence of such commitment means that we do not form in ourselves dispositions to bring about the undesirable effects we have merely caused.

This explanation of what lies behind the doctrine of double effect, though brief, should go some way towards making sense of it. It is not a mere 'casuistical device' for putting a fair face on dubious courses of action. On the contrary, it rests on certain deep truths about what is required for living well.

Of course the doctrine should not be taken to imply that provided that we do not intend what we cause to happen we can always go ahead with actions which bring about foreseen side effects, however undesirable they may be. As we have already noted, we are excused from blame for causing undesirable side effects only if what we are intending to do is something sufficiently important or necessary.

People who do not understand or who reject the truths underlying the doctrine of double effect are apt to say that it merely serves a mask for hypocrisy. In saying this they mean that doctors who really intend to kill their patients in administering doses of morphine can claim that death was merely a foreseen side effect. But there are limits to the extent to which doctors can get away with such lies. Doses which are sufficient to kill a patient are often demonstrably in excess of what is required to control a particular patient's pain. The more clearly pain control standards are refined the less room there will be for devious practice. In any case, the fact that some devious doctors may misuse the doctrine of double effect is no reason why conscientious doctors should not continue to rely on it.

Terminal sedation

In some relatively rare cases a terminally ill patient's pain or acute distress cannot be controlled in a way compatible with the patient remaining conscious. In general, terminal care aims, where possible, to help patients live in a mentally alert fashion, so that they can continue to converse with relatives and friends. To remain mentally alert while dying enables one to attend to duties one may hitherto have ignored: to be reconciled to those from whom one has been estranged and to be reconciled to God in the sacrament of Confession. It is a blessing while dying to be able consciously to receive

Our Lord in communion and to be able to pray. If, however, one is suffering from extreme pain, which is unresponsive to standard pain control measures and which overwhelms consciousness, or if one is suffering from what is called 'terminal anguish', a state of extreme mental torment, these desirable activities are impossible. Relief for the patient's condition can be achieved only by sedating the patient until he is comatose and keeping him comatose until he dies. This is what is known as 'terminal sedation'.

The Church recognises the acceptability of depriving a person of consciousness where there is a serious reason, while emphasising that only a serious reason can justify such a course of action.[27]

Today, however, an increasing number of people are advocating the use of terminal sedation as an 'alternative' to euthanasia or as an interim measure until euthanasia is legalised. It is clear, however, from what they have in mind, that the terminal sedation they recommend is just a version of euthanasia. For what is proposed is:

• that anyone who is terminally ill and who, for whatever reason, wishes to put an end to conscious experience of his or her existence, should be rendered comatose, and...

• that the person should *not* be provided with food and fluids precisely in order to hasten death.

It is clear that this is just slow-motion euthanasia.

When thinking about what is obligatory in the care and treatment of terminally ill patients, we need to distinguish between those who have weeks and months to live and those, on the other hand, who are in what is called the 'terminal phase' of their illness, i.e. have only a few days in which to live.

As we have seen, it is only extreme and relatively rare conditions which justify terminal sedation. Generally, these conditions arise only in the terminal phase of dying. In the terminal phase many patients are disinclined to take anything very much in the way of food and fluids, though they appreciate having their mouths kept moist. If it is quite clear that a comatose patient can be expected to die in a matter of days there is no good case for inserting tubes into the patient to deliver nutrition and fluids. If, however, there were strong and compelling reasons for sedating a patient who had not yet entered the terminal phase of dying, there would be an obligation to tube feed that patient and to provide fluids. Food and fluids, as we have already noted, are not medical treatment which one might judge futile because they can no longer secure a cure or palliate symptoms. They are needed simply to sustain life and as such are primary ingredients of that basic care owing to living human beings. You cannot say you are 'letting nature take its course' if what you are allowing to happen is death through dehydration and starvation owing to your neglect.

To summarise: there are particular and relatively rare circumstances in which the use of terminal sedation is consistent with what the Church teaches about our duties to the terminally ill. However, what is being promoted nowadays as a desirable practice of terminal sedation is simply a form of euthanasia.

Advance Directives

As we saw in the introductory section of this booklet, in defining terms, 'advance directives' may take two forms. A person who wishes to determine what should and should not happen to him in the way of treatment and care when he becomes incompetent, may go about doing so in one or other of two ways. Either he may confer on someone a continuing power of attorney, appointing that person to make decisions on his behalf if and when he becomes incompetent; or he may make out a written advance declaration, indicating his wishes. The first approach would have no legal effect in English law at present, though the Government plans legislation to provide for continuing powers of attorney in respect of healthcare matters. The second approach is at present more effective, since judicial decisions seem to have recognised the authority of advance directives, at least that type of advance directive which is in effect an *advance refusal of treatment*. While doctors cannot be obliged to do what in their judgment it is inappropriate to do, it is held that they are obliged to *refrain* from doing what patients have declared in advance they do not wish done to them.

It is clear that someone who is given a continuing power of attorney may use it to decline treatment on one's behalf precisely to end one's life, and that advance refusals of treatment may be designed to ensure that death is hastened in circumstances in which one judges that life would no longer be worthwhile.

Clearly if we are to give a person continuing powers of attorney in respect of our medical care, if and when we are incompetent, we should have solid reasons for thinking that the person entrusted with those powers will act in a morally acceptable fashion and will seek to ensure that nothing is done or omitted in our care and treatment with a view to ending our lives.

There are a number of formats for advance declarations in circulation, of which the best known is probably the one circulated by the Voluntary Euthanasia Society. The formulation of most such declarations (and certainly that of the VES) is designed to accommodate euthanasiast refusals of treatment and care; that is, refusals by people who think that if they were to end their days with, say, dementia, their lives would be no longer worthwhile, whereas refusal of treatment or care, if complied with, would serve to hasten their deaths.

It should be clear that anyone who recognises the truth of the Church's teaching about euthanasia and suicide should avoid use of advance directives of the kind circulated by the VES.

People often argue that respect for autonomy requires respect for advance directives which clearly state a desire for euthanasia by omission of treatment or care. But there are limits to the respect owing to autonomy, and particularly clear limits when the person for whom one is responsible has ceased to be autonomous. The point has been well made in the following terms:

> What is characteristically missing in much modern discussion of autonomy and self-determination is any strong sense that the most fundamental expression of respect for the dignity of human beings is not respect for autonomy but respect for the good of human beings. When persons have exercisable capacities for self-determination then respect for their self-determination is integral to respect for their good as persons: for it is in and through choice that they have the possibility of shaping their characters for good (or ill). But when persons do not yet, or no longer, possess presently exercisable capacities for self-determination, self-determination cannot be an essential ingredient, so to speak, in what one respects in respecting their good. Any exercise of self-determination which seeks to determine what should (or should not) happen to one, if and when one comes to be incompetent, should be respected only to the extent that doing so is consistent with respecting the good of the now incompetent patient.[28]

Footnotes

23. Congregation for the Doctrine of the Faith, Declaration on Euthanasia *Iura et Bona* (5 May 1980), II: *AAS* 72 (1980), 546.

24. Pope John Paul II, *Evangelium Vitae* 3, 65.

25. *In the 'best interests' of the patient* (forthcoming).

26. For some of the evidence see Luke Gormally (ed.) *Euthanasia, Clinical Practice and the Law*. London: The Linacre Centre 1994, pp. 15-19.

27. See Congregation for the Doctrine of the Faith, Declaration on Euthanasia *Iura et Bona*, Vatican City: Libreria Editrice Vaticana 1980, pp. 8-9, quoting Pope Pius XII, *Address* (24.02.1957), 49 (1957) *Acta Apostolicae Sedis*: 129-147.

28. Luke Gormally (ed.), *Euthanasia, Clinical Practice and the Law*, pp. 146-147.

SOURCES OF CHURCH TEACHING ON SUICIDE AND EUTHANASIA

Whenever the Church teaches it considers itself a medium, and not a creator, of moral truth. That is to say, the Church does not invent the moral teaching it proclaims but merely passes on that which it has received. Any Pope would confirm that he does not have the authority to change the moral law that has been received. Any moral truth the Church defends has its roots in the objective moral order, mediated to us by the Church's authoritative interpretation of the sources of our knowledge of that moral order. Those sources are: first, the Bible; secondly, the apostolic teaching of Christians throughout the ages; and thirdly, natural law, already discussed in Chapter 3. This brief survey of the sources of the contemporary Church's teaching will therefore review first the biblical witness and then the witness of tradition.

The Bible on suicide, homicide and euthanasia

Suicide is several times referred to in the Bible; however, it is nowhere described as something morally acceptable. One reference to euthanasia or 'mercy-killing' lies in the request of the wounded King Saul that he be killed before he falls into the hands of his enemies. In the first book of Samuel, this request is refused, and Saul then falls upon his sword (*1 Sam* 31:5-6). In the second book of Samuel, a young man reports to King David that he has killed Saul at his own request (*2 Sam* 1:6-10). Despite the fact that, in the young man's story, Saul was mortally wounded and had asked for death, he is severely punished by King David for what he claims to have done (*2 Sam* 1:11-27).

In the Bible, life is seen as something to respect, even when it is beset with suffering. The whole of the book of Job testifies to this; but there are also many places where the faith that does not despair in the face of suffering is commended. For example: I kept my faith even when I said, 'I am greatly afflicted' (*Ps* 116:10).

It is clear therefore that suffering is not something that leads inevitably to despair but rather the place where God is known most powerfully. It is those who suffer that Our Lord singles out for the blessings of the beatitudes (*Matt* 5:2-10). Throughout the whole of the Bible there is a preference expressed for those who are most weak and vulnerable. These are always given a special place in God's protective heart. In the Bible God is frequently referred to as the "goel", which is often translated as 'the redeemer', but which bears the more exact meaning 'the defender of the innocent' (cf. *Gn* 4:9-15; *Is* 41:14; *Jer* 50:34; *Ps* 19:14).[29] In the Bible, as well as in Church teaching, there is a recognition of the inherent value of human life.

There is clearly found in Scripture the injunction against murder: You shall not kill (*Exodus* 20:13; *Matt* 19:18). It is evident from other biblical texts that the commandment does not exclude killing in war and the killing of those who have committed capital crimes and so some translations read: "You shall not commit murder," by which is meant the intentional killing of the innocent. It is implicit within this commandment that the killing of one's own self is equally prohibited. This is brought out even more clearly if we consider the positive command: You shall love your neighbour as yourself (*Mt* 19:19: *Rm* 13:9). Implicit within this command is the assumption that self-love is a natural and noble attitude. That is why, as we shall see below, St Thomas understands suicide as chiefly a sin against charity: that is to say, it demonstrates a lack of the love that we owe ourselves as creatures created in the image and likeness of God.

Furthermore, it is apparent that the current idea of ownership over one's life and body is also an idea foreign to Scripture. It is God alone who reserves the right to exercise authority over life and death:

> See now that I, even I, am he, and there is no god beside me; I kill and I make alive; I wound and I heal; and there is none that can deliver out of my hand. (*Dt* 32:39)

And as St Paul writes: You are not your own. You were bought with a price (*1 Cor* 6:19,20). It is clear then that neither the argument from mercy, nor the argument from self-determination, can find a foothold in scripture. In the Bible we find a call to respect human life, and to acknowledge the duty we owe to God and to our neighbour never to despair, even when we are "greatly afflicted".

Witnesses to the tradition on suicide and euthanasia

The Didache

Once we move beyond the biblical literature we find an even more direct attack on the ideas that are prevalent within our own culture. In the *Didache*, a work attributed to the apostles and one of the earliest pieces of non-Biblical Christian literature, we find a contrast that is reasserted in the most recent teaching of John Paul II in *Evangelium Vitae*:

(1) There are two Ways, a Way of Life and a Way of Death and the difference between these two Ways is great. The Way of Life is this: Thou shalt love first the Lord thy Creator, and secondly thy neighbour as thyself; and thou shalt do nothing to any man that thou wouldst not wish to be done to thyself... (2) The second commandment in the Teaching means: Commit no murder, adultery, sodomy, fornication, or theft. Practise no magic, sorcery, abortion or infanticide... (5) The Way of Death is this... In it are murders, adulteries, lusts, fornications... Here are those who persecute good

men, hold truth in abhorrence, and love falsehood...
Gentleness and patience are beyond their conception...
they show no compassion for the poor, they do not
suffer with the suffering, they do not acknowledge their
Creator... they drive away the needy, oppress the
suffering, they are advocates of the rich and unjust
judges of the poor; they are filled with every sin. May
you be able to stay ever apart, O children, from all
these sins![30]

Here we find the call to true compassion, the call to
"suffer with the suffering". We do not find the peculiar
claim that, in the name of mercy, the suffering should be
killed. Such thinking clearly belongs to the "Way of Death".

St Augustine

Euthanasia is even more explicitly condemned in the
writings of St Augustine (354-430). Although he does not
use the term euthanasia it is startling how relevant his
words are to our current situation:

It is never licit to kill another: even if he should
wish it, indeed if he request it because, hanging
between life and death, he begs for help in freeing the
soul struggling against the bonds of the body and
longing to be released; nor is it licit even when a sick
person is no longer able to live.[31]

Here, St Augustine, in the first millennium of the
Christian era, condemns any attempt to justify killing by

an appeal to the right of self-determination. It is clear to him, as to many others, that it is not possible for anyone to lay aside the prohibition against killing, even if the person killed consents to the crime. Its character as an intrinsically immoral act is not altered by the complicity of the victim. For the same reason suicide is condemned:

> ...the law, rightly interpreted, even prohibits suicide, where it says, 'Thou shalt not kill.' This is proved especially by the omission of the words 'thy neighbour'... For the love of our neighbour is regulated by the love of ourselves, as it is written, 'Thou shalt love thy neighbour as thyself'...how much greater reason have we to understand that a man may not kill himself, since in the commandment, 'Thou shalt not kill', there is no limitation added nor any exception made in favour of any one, and least of all in favour of him on whom the command is laid.[32]

St Thomas Aquinas

We meet the same argument as the one presented above in the works of St Thomas Aquinas (1225-1274), who states, in agreement with St Augustine:

> It is altogether unlawful to kill oneself... because everything naturally loves itself, the result being that everything naturally keeps itself in being, and resists corruptions so far as it can. Wherefore suicide is contrary to the inclination of nature, and to charity

whereby every man should love himself. Hence suicide is always a mortal sin, as being contrary to the natural law and to charity.[33]

Again, St Thomas points out that the wrongness of suicide resides in the fact that a person is demonstrating a lack of proper love for self. He also points to a further reason why suicide is wrong, one we have not considered in detail in this booklet but which is nevertheless clearly relevant and important. Suicide is wrong, he states:

> ...because every part, as such, belongs to the whole. Now every man is part of the community, and so, as such, he belongs to the community. Hence by killing himself he injures the community...[34]

In considering suicide we should bear in mind that suffering patients, although they may consider their desire to die as one that only affects themselves, are part of a community and often part of a family. The patient has duties to that community, including the duty of acting in ways consistent with human worth and dignity; every act which is an assault on human dignity is liable to damage both the perception of, and respect for, human dignity in one's community. Advocates of suicide and euthanasia, who defend them as 'private acts' which do no harm to others, are radically mistaken. The damage done to the community is even clearer in the case of euthanasia than in that of suicide, for the person requesting euthanasia wants someone else to do the killing. Hence someone else is directly corrupted by the carrying out of euthanasiast killing. Since it is doctors who are generally expected to do this it is doctors who are corrupted by euthanasia. Since trust in the good dispositions of doctors is necessary for good healthcare, and since healthcare is an important part of the common good of society, the corruption of doctors is profoundly damaging to the common good.

As well as recognising that suicide is contrary to charity and the commandment to "love your neighbour as yourself", St Thomas also stresses that suicide is an offence against the rightful ownership God has over our lives. He says, in accord with Scripture, that:

> ...life is God's gift to man, and is subject to His power, Who kills and makes to live. Hence whoever takes his own life, sins against God...For it belongs to God alone to pronounce sentence of death and life, according to *Dt* 32:39, 'I will kill and I will make to live'.[35]

St Thomas affirms that our lives are not our own. We do not have the rights of an owner over our lives, but only the duties of a steward.

St Thomas also anticipates the current argument that makes appeal to a right of self-determination. He first presents the argument itself before he replies to it:

> It would seem lawful for a man to kill himself. For murder is a sin in so far as it is contrary to justice. But

no man can do an injustice to himself...Therefore no man sins by killing himself.[36]

This seems to be exactly the sort of argument that is presented when an appeal to the right of self-determination is made. Those who use the argument might even agree that the intentional killing of the innocent is wrong when it deprives them unjustly of their life. But they would argue that a person cannot commit an injustice against his own self since whatever he chooses to do must, by its very nature, be in his own interests. St Thomas resists this by repeating an argument already referred to, namely that the chief case against suicide is not that it is unjust but that it is contrary to a proper love of self:

> Murder is a sin, not only because it is contrary to justice, but also because it is opposed to charity which a man should have towards himself: in this respect suicide is a sin in relation to oneself.[37]

This is St Thomas's response to the argument based on an appeal to self-determination; he goes on to answer the argument based on an appeal to mercy:

> Man is made master of himself through his free-will: wherefore he can lawfully dispose of himself as to those matters which pertain to this life which is ruled by man's free-will. But the passage from this life to another and happier one is subject not to man's free-will but to the power of God. Hence it is not lawful for

man to take his own life that he may pass to a happier life, nor that he may escape any unhappiness whatsoever of the present life, because the ultimate and most fearsome evil of this life is death... Therefore to bring death upon oneself in order to escape the other afflictions of this life, is to adopt a greater evil in order to avoid a lesser.[38]

Thus we see that St Thomas opposes suicide firstly because it usurps the rule of God and secondly, because it does not demonstrate the required fundamental loyalty to life that flows from the duty to love oneself. These arguments are also clearly relevant to assessing the disposition of the will of the person who requests euthanasia. Euthanasia itself, as an act carried out by a person other than the one who dies, falls under the general condemnation of murder as an act of grave injustice, for, as we have seen, the reason for euthanasia (that someone's life is judged to be not worthwhile) is radically incompatible with justice.

Footnotes

29. *Evangelium Vitae* 53.

30. *Didache*, I, 1; II, 1-2; V, 1 and 3: *Patres Apostolici*, ed. F.X. Funk, I, 2-3, 6-9, 14-17; cf. Letter of Pseudo-Barnabas, XIX, 5: *loc. cit.*, 90-93.

31. St Augustine, Letter 204, 5.

32. St Augustine, *De Civitate Dei* I, 20.

33. St Thomas Aquinas, *Summa theologiae* IIa IIae, q.64, a.5.

34. *Ibid.*

35. *Ibid.*

36. *Ibid.*

37. *Ibid.*

38. St Thomas Aquinas *Summa theologiae* IIa IIae, q.6, a.5.

CONCLUSION

The Church unequivocally opposes euthanasia. Some would try to obscure this straightforward teaching by referring to the complexities acknowledged in this booklet of deciding when some action or omission is, in fact, euthanasia. However, despite some practical complexities, the meaning of euthanasia remains essentially simple since it relies upon concepts that are readily understandable:

> Euthanasia's terms of reference, therefore, are to be found in the intention of the will and in the methods used.[39]

If your intention is to cause death because of a judgement made concerning the quality of a person's life then euthanasia is what you have in mind in acting or refraining from action. If your intention is something else entirely - for example, to treat the patient's pain, or to spare him or her some burdensome procedure - your choice will not be euthanasia, even if it may hasten death.

The intrinsic wrongness of suicide and euthanasia

Advocacy of suicide and euthanasia is wrong because it makes several fundamental errors of judgement. First, it fails to recognise that the lives of all human beings have a distinctive value and dignity. Secondly, it fails to recognise that our lives are not our own to dispose of at will, since this is contrary both to the love of self which is proper to our nature and contrary to God's sovereignty. Third, it illustrates an attitude toward human life and suffering that is conditioned by a society that places too much value on productivity and usefulness and is increasingly forgetting what it means to be present to those who suffer. Finally, it is a contravention of the fifth commandment: "Thou shalt not kill." The force of this commandment is not lessened if the person killed is complicit in the killing.

The damaging effects of euthanasia

Apart from its intrinsic wrongness, it would be an error to presume that euthanasia would bring the benefits claimed for it. There are again a number of concerns that every person should have if tempted to condone euthanasia in certain cases.

For example, if it is allowed that some human lives lack value then a truly enormous concession has been made. For the basic value and dignity possessed by every human being is the foundation of our entitlement to justice, and therefore, among other things, the right not to be unjustly killed. If it is truly the case that human lives can be judged to lack value and basic dignity, whether or not a person consents to being killed becomes something of an irrelevance. A legal order which allows that human beings may be killed because they lack worthwhile lives has abandoned the foundations of justice and therefore abandoned in principle the non-discriminatory protection of its subjects. The way is therefore open to further arbitrary extensions of the judgment that certain human lives are not worthwhile. It would not be surprising if pressure is placed, in the future, on the old and infirm to offer themselves for euthanasia as if it were somehow the duty of those who are not productive to stop using up essential resources. Advocates of euthanasia are liable to dismiss any type of 'slippery slope' argument. But history testifies that slippery slopes can become very slippery indeed, and laws that have been introduced as mere exceptions have been used, time and again, as the first step in larger and more sweeping developments. The abortion laws in this country are a case in point; we now have what in practice is abortion on demand.

Furthermore, it is perfectly understandable that we should slide down the slope once we have moved off the level ground since it is where the logic of the move that we have made inevitably takes us.

The only appropriate standpoint is that of insistence on the value and inviolability of every human life and a commitment unconditionally to promote the Gospel of Life.

"This day I call heaven and earth as witnesses against you that I have set before you life and death, blessings and curses. Now choose life, so that you and your children may live..." (*Dt* 30:19)

Footnotes

39. Congregation for the Doctrine of the Faith, Declaration on Euthanasia *Iura et Bona* (5 May 1980), II: *AAS* 72 (1980), 546.

Further Reading

Church documents

These documents are available from the CTS.

Congregation for the Doctrine of the Faith, *Declaration on Euthanasia* [known by the first two words of the Latin text *Iura et Bona*] 1980.

Pope John Paul II, Encyclical Letter *Evangelium Vitae* ['The Gospel of Life'].

Bioethics texts

Luke Gormally (ed.), *Euthanasia, Clinical Practice and the Law*. London: The Linacre Centre 1994.

Helen Watt, *Life and Death in Healthcare Ethics*: *A short introduction*. London: Routledge 2000.

John Keown (ed.), *Euthanasia Examined: ethical, clinical and legal perspectives*. Cambridge: Cambridge University Press 1995 (paperback edition 1997). This book includes both pro-euthanasia and anti-euthanasia contributions.

John Keown, *Euthanasia, Ethics and Public Policy. An Argument against Legalisation*. Cambridge: Cambridge University Press 2002. This book discusses case-law and legislation which favours euthanasia.